WriteTraits®

STUDENT TRAITBOOK

Vicki Spandel • Jeff Hicks

GREAT SOURCE®
EDUCATION GROUP
A Houghton Mifflin Company

Vicki Spandel

Vicki Spandel was codirector of the original teacher team that developed the six-trait model and has designed instructional materials for all grade levels. She has written several books, including *Creating Writers–Linking Writing Assessment and Instruction* (Longman), and is a former language arts teacher, journalist, technical writer, consultant, and scoring director for dozens of state, county, and district writing assessments.

Jeff Hicks

Jeff Hicks has over 17 years of teaching experience in grades two through nine. Until recently, Jeff taught seventh/eighth grade English and math on a two-person teaching team, focusing on the reading/writing connection through six-trait writing activities. Currently, Jeff is a full-time writer and presenter.

Design/Production: Bill Westwood/Andy Cox, David Drury

Illustration: Jim Higgins, Mark DaGrossa, Scott Van Buren, Chris Vallo

Proofreading/Editorial: Erik Martin/Judy Bernheim, Alex Culpepper

Cover: Illustration by Claude Martinot Design

Printed in the United States of America

International Standard Book Number: 0-669-49038-5

5 6 7 8 9 10 - PO - 07 06 05 04

Contents

Unit 1: Ideas

Unit 2: Organization

Unit 3: Voice

Unit 4: Word Choice

Unit 5: Sentence Fluency

Unit 6: Conventions

Warm-up Activity

Ranking Three Papers

Read the three writing samples that follow. Decide which sample is strongest, which sample is next strongest, and which sample is weakest. Each sample is about Bristles the dog and a trip to the swimming pool.

Sample 1

I was almost to the pool when I remembered I had forgotten my radio. I like to bring a radio with me so that we can listen to music when we are swimming. My friend Bill is the best swimmer of all of us. Anyway, I was heading back for the radio when this huge dog named Bristles came out of nowhere, barking and growling like mad. He is our neighbor's dog, and he's supposed to be on a leash. Lucky for me, a guy came out with a rake and chased him away, so I did not get hurt. When I finally got to the pool, most of my friends were already there. The only one who didn't come was Brad because he had to go to the dentist. We sure got hungry, but we all stopped for tacos on our way home. I thought about getting an extra one for that maniac dog Bristles, but I didn't. I'm taking lessons next month so that I can be a lifeguard one day.

Sample 2

Last week, as I was headed to the neighborhood swimming pool, Bristles the dog decided to run out and greet me. He snarled, baring his teeth. He was drooling and smelled especially rank, even for Bristles. I wanted to wave my arms at him to scare him away, but I was overloaded with stuff like towels, suntan lotion, swim fins, and my Dad's old radio. Running away wouldn't have helped either because I would have dropped all that junk. I couldn't have outrun Bristles anyway. He's smelly, but he sure can run fast. He kept circling me, moving closer, drooling and growling. Just as I thought I was going to be Bristles's lunch, Mr. Wheeler, the neighbor's gardener, came around the corner waving his rake and shouting at Bristles. Amazingly, Bristles turned and trotted to his backyard. Mr. Wheeler winked at me. I tried winking back, but I was wearing my swim goggles, so I doubt he saw anything. I gave him my best smile, though, and then trudged off for the pool.

Sample 3

On Tuesday, I was headed for the pool to meet my friends, and my arms were loaded down with stuff for the pool. So I couldn't really do much when Bristles came charging out at me. He was growling and circling around me, and I thought for sure I was a goner! Just then, something amazing happened. The Johnstons' gardener, Mr. Wheeler, came around the side of the house, and he saw that I was having a hard time with Bristles. He waved his rake and yelled for the dog to go home. And Bristles did go home! I could not believe it. Later at the pool, I told my friends about what had happened, and they told me that I should carry something with me to feed Bristles. That is a good idea, but it isn't always handy to have an old hot dog or something in your pocket. I don't even have pockets in my swimsuit!

Share Your Thoughts

Rate the samples. Be sure to add your reasons.

Sample _____ is the strongest because

_____.

Sample _____ is the next strongest because

_____.

Sample _____ is the weakest because

_____.

Unit 1 Ideas

Sometimes writers try to include too many ideas in their writing. When this happens, the writing might remind readers of a garage sale: a little of this, some of that, and no one thing in particular. Strong writing isn't like a garage sale. It's more like an advertisement for one thing. An ad for a car, for example, doesn't try to sell anything but that car. It focuses on one product—and it gives details that will make you want to buy that car. You could say it has a main idea and all the details needed to keep you interested.

To help you make the best of your good ideas, you'll learn about

◆ narrowing the topic

◆ staying focused on the main topic

◆ choosing the best details

◆ including all the information a reader needs

name: _____ date: _____

Taming the Wild Topic

It's time to do some writing in your classroom, and everyone gets to choose a topic. Suppose your good friend has chosen "The Eating Habits of the Australian Python." You have chosen "Animals." Who will have the toughest time writing a clear, focused main idea? Probably you will—your topic is too big! With a topic as broad as "Animals," your writing will either be too general—"Animals are everywhere. Some are big, some are small"—or as detailed as an encyclopedia, with paragraphs on everything from apes to zebras. Now consider your friend's topic. With a focused topic like "Eating Habits of the Australian Python," it's simple to know just what details to include.

Pushing It Through the Funnel

When a topic is too large, it's hard to know where to start writing. If you find yourself in this situation, imagine yourself pushing your topic through a funnel. Many ideas can fit into the wide end, but a more manageable idea comes out the narrow end. Think of this as taming your topic.

Taming "Animals"

To tame a big topic, ask yourself some questions about it. Start your questions with key words such as *Who, What, When, Where, Why, How, Which,* and *Is.* Keep asking yourself questions until your topic becomes more manageable. Each question and answer narrows the topic and pushes it farther down the funnel.

Question: *What* do I really want to say about animals?

Answer: I want to say that I really like some animals.

(Hint: If your answer to this question is "I don't know" it's time to ask another question. It may even be time to change directions completely.)

Topic Tamed? ___ Yes _X_ No

Question: *Which* animals do I like?

Answer: I like animals that hunt, have claws, and have big teeth.

Topic Tamed? ___ Yes _X_ No

Question: *Is* there *one* particular animal I want to write about?

Answer: Yes, I like the snow leopard. I've always thought the snow leopard was cool.

Topic Tamed? ___ Yes _X_ No (But you're getting close.)

Question: *What* do I want to tell readers about the snow leopard?

Answer: I want to describe how the snow leopard hunts and what it hunts.

Topic Tamed? _X_ Yes ___ No

Your Response

Has the topic been tamed?

___ Yes ___ No

To answer this question, imagine a box big enough to "hold" your topic. Is there a box large enough to hold "Animals" as a topic? Probably not, and if there were, it would be too large to lift. Is there a box big enough to hold the topic "Hunting Like a Snow Leopard"?

You Ask the Questions

Work with a partner to make the general topic "Fish" more manageable. One of you will ask *Who, What, When, Where, Why, How, Which,* and *Is* questions about the topic, and the other will answer the questions. After each question and answer, decide whether you have tamed the topic. When you have a workable topic, write it at the end of the funnel.

Question: _____

Answer: _____

Topic Tamed? ____ Yes ____ No

Question: _____

Answer: _____

Topic Tamed? ____ Yes ____ No

Question: _____

Answer: _____

Topic Tamed? ____ Yes ____ No

You Are the Tamer

Choose a topic, ask the questions, provide the answers, and decide when the topic has been tamed. When you are finished, write the tamed topic on the line at the end of the funnel.

Topic: _____

Question: _____

Answer: _____

Topic Tamed? ____ Yes ____ No

Question: _____

Answer: _____

Topic Tamed? ____ Yes ____ No

Question: _____

Answer: _____

Topic Tamed? ____ Yes ____ No

A Writer's Question

Do you think the funneling activity is something you could do by yourself with your own writing topics?

I couldn't do this. Help. ____

I could "funnel" with a little help from a partner. ____

I am ready to "funnel" on my own. ____

Lesson 2

name: .... date: ....

Targeted Writing

Quality writing always has a clear main idea that is easy to understand. It is the reason for the writing. Writing without a main idea is like a pile of bricks with no mortar to hold them together. Writing that does not have a clear main idea frustrates readers as they try to understand what the writer wants to say.

Finding the Main Idea

Read Sample 1. Ask yourself, *What is the author's main idea?*

Hint: Is it possible that this author hasn't settled on a main idea yet?

Sample 1

My friend Scott's family is making their house bigger because they're going to have a baby in October. That's not the best time to be born. What if your birthday was on Halloween? People might forget about it because of all the pumpkin carving, costume making, and candy buying that goes on. I love candy. This one friend of mine, Matthew, has his birthday on Christmas. His parents just give him one present for both days. That would make me feel bad, like my birthday wasn't important. My teacher says a kid is supposed to feel important. It's called self-esteem. I think I have lots of self-esteem, and that's a good thing. I'm also good at baseball.

Your Thoughts

Did you find a main idea for this paragraph?

_____ Yes _____ No

Explain your answer.

_____

_____

_____

_____

Now read Sample 2. As you read it, compare it to Sample 1. See whether you can find this author's main idea.

Sample 2

It was so hot at my school the other day, I thought I would melt into my chair. Our school doesn't have any air conditioning, so my teacher brought in a big fan. She also kept the blinds closed, but it didn't help much. Some kids complained all day, "It's so-o-o hot, Mrs. Elarth." Did they think saying it out loud would make it any cooler? Other kids kept asking whether we could go outside. What were they thinking? There's not much shade outside, and there wasn't any wind. If we had gone out, someone would have fainted or just melted. Mrs. Elarth kept her cool (ha-ha!) through all this, which was more than I could have done if I had been in charge. Maybe what we need are "Sun" days, like "Snow" days except that it's too hot to be in school.

Your Thoughts

Did you find a main idea for Sample 2?

_____ Yes _____ No

If you answered YES, go back and underline the sentence that you think comes *closest* to giving you the writer's main idea.

The Bull's-eye

One way to see whether you have found a main idea is to think of your writing as a circular target. Think of the bull's-eye as your main idea and all the circles around it as details supporting the main idea. Look at the graphic organizer. Notice how the details in the circles all connect and support the writer's main idea about a really hot day at school.

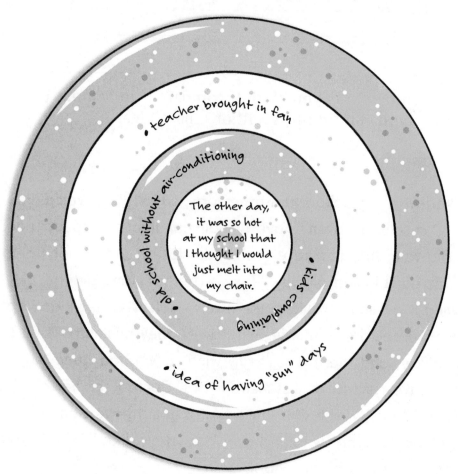

Strong Details for a Big Bull's-eye

Here's a chance to use the bull's-eye and target sketch as a method of prewriting. Choose a topic. Put your main idea in the bull's-eye. Put the details in the circles. Add more detail circles if you need to.

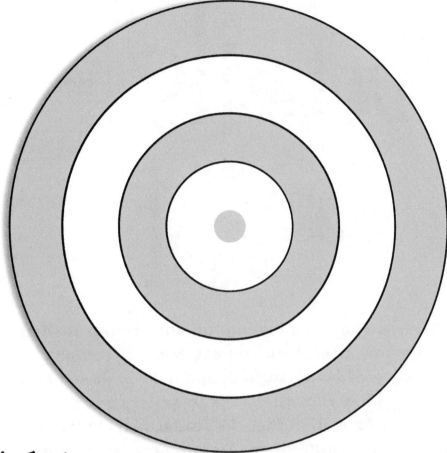

Your Target

Now, use the main idea and supporting details from your target to write a short paragraph.

_____

_____

_____

_____

_____

A Writer's Question

Did writing from your target sketch help you stay "targeted" on your main idea? Read your paragraph aloud to a partner and find out. Ask your partner, _Can you identify my main idea? Do my supporting details relate to my main idea?_

Lesson 2 **15**

name: .... date: ....

Details on a Diet

The difference between feeling full and feeling stuffed depends on how much food you eat. Most of us don't like the feeling of being stuffed, and neither do readers. Strong writing has enough details to satisfy a reader but not so much information that the reader feels "stuffed." Remember that a "stuffed" reader will stop reading in self-defense, so put those details "on a diet." Make every detail count!

Sorting It Out: On or Off the Plate?

Imagine that you are writing a piece to educate readers about frogs. What details will you choose? Some details on the following list are things your readers will probably find important and interesting. These details go "on the plate." Other details are not important or particularly interesting, or they may be things everyone already knows. These details should be "off the plate."

As you read the list, decide what to keep on the plate and what to toss off the plate. Circle the number of each detail you would put on the plate.

Details About Frogs

1. Frogs are ectotherms—their body temperature depends on the temperature around them.

2. Frogs can hop or jump.

3. Frogs communicate by croaking.

4. Frogs come in different sizes.

5. There are over 4,000 species of frogs.

6. Most frogs eat insects.

7. Frog legs can be eaten by humans.

8. Frogs grow from tadpoles or pollywogs.

9. Tadpoles live in water.

10. Scientists have found frog fossils from the Jurassic Period (144–208 million years ago).

11. Frogs are amphibians, so they live on land and in water.

12. Toads, newts, and salamanders are amphibians.

13. Frogs live on land and water.

14. Frogs and toads are amphibians called anurans.

15. There is a book called *Frog and Toad*.

16. Frogs catch insects with their tongues.

17. Frogs live all over the world.

18. Frogs do not drink.

19. Frogs absorb water through their skin.

20. When frogs are on land, they can dry out.

21. Bats, turtles, herons, snakes, tarantulas, and other animals eat frogs.

22. Frogs jump so that they can move fast without leaving a trail.

23. There are male and female frogs.

24. A frog uses its eyes to help push food down its throat.

25. Frogs can be green or other colors.

26. Many frogs live near water.

27. Frogs usually have long legs.

28. A frog has teeth in its upper jaw.

Share and Compare

After you finish selecting the best of the details, meet with a partner to compare lists. Did you fill your "plates" with the same details? If you didn't, take a few minutes to discuss the items each of you chose to put "on the plate."

Using Your "Plates" to Write

Take one more look at the items you circled. Begin a paragraph about frogs, using the circled details from your list. Use about six items that you put "on the plate." (Suggestion: If you know something about frogs that is not on the list but should be, go ahead and use it. Just be sure that it's important or interesting enough to be "on the plate.") When you finish, be prepared to share your work with a partner or with the class.

name: .... date: ....

A Writer's Question

When you have a lot to say about a topic, it's hard to leave out information. How did you decide what to circle or not to circle on the list of facts about frogs?

_____

_____

_____

Lesson 4

Filling in the Details

Imagine arriving at school late. Everyone in class is working on something involving colored paper and glue, but you can't tell what they're making. Because your head is buzzing with questions, you need to have someone answer them for you.

Similarly, when you write, you need to fill in the details so that readers have a clear picture of what you want to say. Writers must think like readers. Writers must ask themselves, *Where are the holes in my writing? What information do I need to fill in?*

Sharing an Example: Harris and Me

When authors introduce a new character, they want readers to understand what that character is like and to connect their own lives to that character's life. Clear details help readers do this. But what if an author forgets to fill in the details? Read this version of a passage from Gary Paulsen's *Harris and Me.* Gary Paulsen's original description of Louie has been changed a little. What picture does it create in your mind?

Sample 1

Details Left Out

An old man sat at the table in his coat. He was really dirty. His beard was filled with bits of stuff. He had blue eyes and no teeth.

Louie.

Your Response

What kind of picture do these words create for you?

_____ I'm still in the dark.

_____ I know a few things but it's still fuzzy.

_____ It's a clear picture. Louie is real to me.

Now, read the sample the way the author wrote it in the book.

Sample 2

The Original

At the end of the table sat an old man in a wool coat—though it was summer and hot in the kitchen from the wood stove on which the pancakes were cooking—a man so incredibly dirty that it was hard to find a patch of skin on his face or neck not covered with soil or grease. He wore a matted beard—stuck with bits of dirt and sawdust and what looked like (and I found later to be) dried manure and dribble spit and tobacco juice. All this around two piercingly blue gun-barrel eyes and a toothless mouth.

Louie.

Gary Paulsen. *Harris and Me.* (New York: Bantam Doubleday Dell Books, 1993) pp. 14–15

Your Response

Now what kind of picture do you have of Louie? Use the space on the following page to write two or three details from this sample that you think are particularly clear.

_____

_____

_____

_____

_____

_____

Holes

You might call Sample 1 "Swiss cheese" writing because it has a lot of holes in it.

Let's see whether you can fill in the holes, just as author Gary Paulsen did. Read the next passage. Make a list of what information needs to be included.

Uncle Anthony

My Uncle Anthony is a great guy. He's tall and always wears a hat. When he comes to visit, we have a lot of fun. He travels all over for his job. He brings me stuff from every trip.

My List of Holes

1. Why was he a great guy? _____

2. _____

3. _____

4. _____

5. _____

6. _____

Filling in the Holes

To fix this writing, you need to fill in the holes. Since you don't really know Uncle Anthony, you will need to use your imagination to create details.

Uncle Anthony—Revised Version

_____

_____

_____

_____

_____

A Writer's Question

How good were you at finding and filling holes? Rate yourself from 1 to 6, with 1 being the lowest, and 6 being the highest.

1	2	3	4	5	6
I'm still not sure how to find the holes.					I'm very confident about finding and filling in the holes.

Organization

Organization is putting things in an order that makes sense. Picture a bookshelf with a row of books held in place by two bookends. Those books are like the main content, or the main message, of your writing. The bookends keep them upright so they don't topple from the shelf. Those bookends are like the lead (beginning) and the conclusion (ending) of your writing. A critical part of organizing anything is deciding where or how to begin and end. If you have a powerful beginning, details that connect to a strong main idea, events in the right order, and a strong ending, then you will be one well-organized writer.

You will be able to write a well-organized piece of writing after you learn about

◆ writing a strong lead

◆ placing information in the best order

◆ sticking to the main idea

◆ writing a strong conclusion

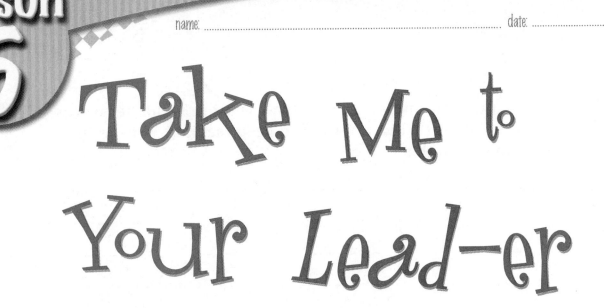

name: .... date: ....

Take Me to Your Lead-er

With so many great books around, writers know they must hook a reader's interest within the first few pages or risk losing that reader to another book. Many writers are able to pull readers in with a good lead, the first few sentences of the story or essay. The first lead a writer creates may not be the best one, though. Good writers often draft several different leads and then choose the one most likely to catch a reader's interest.

Sharing an Example: The Skin I'm In

Read the following lead from writer Sharon G. Flake. As you read, think about how it makes you feel: a little edgy? slightly curious? interested in reading more?

The first time I seen her, I got a bad feeling inside. Not like I was in danger or nothing. Just like she was somebody I should stay clear of. To tell the truth, she was a freak like me. The kind of person folks can't help but tease. That's bad if you're a kid like me. It's worse for a new teacher like her.

Miss Saunders is as different as they come. First off, she got a man's name, Michael. Now who ever heard of a woman named that? She's tall and fat like nobody's business, and she's got the smallest feet I ever seen. Worse yet, she's got a giant white stain spread halfway across her face like somebody tossed acid on it or something.

Sharon G. Flake. *The Skin I'm In.* (New York: Jump at the Sun/Hyperion Books for Children, 1998) p. 1

Your Response

What do you think of this author's lead? How did her words make you feel? Did you want to keep reading? Write your response to this lead here:

_____

_____

_____

_____

Choosing the Lead-er

Following are two possible leads for two different pieces of writing. In each case, read both leads and then decide which one (A or B) would work better and why. Mark your answer.

Two possible leads for a story about a calf

A We live on a ranch with lots of cattle. For some reason, one calf did not want to drink milk from her mother the way a calf usually does. She would get sick if she didn't. My grandpa and dad had to push the mother into a small pen. They milked her into a baby bottle and then fed the calf through the bottle.

B Without her mother's milk, my grandma said our new baby calf would get sick and die. I didn't want that to happen, but the little calf would not snuggle up under her mom and drink—and already she was almost too weak to stand. Grandpa said we would have to do something drastic. He and Dad would herd the nervous mother into the chute and milk her into a bottle for the calf. This was the little calf's only chance, so I sure hoped it would work.

Lead A or B? _____ Why? _____

_____

Two possible leads for a report about snakes

A "Seeing" heat? "Tasting" air? Are these some of the special powers of a new super hero? No! They are just two of the strange things that the pit viper and the eyelash viper can do to help them hunt and defend themselves. Come with me now into the amazing world of snakes.

B Some people think snakes are really scary. Some people think snakes are really cool. This report will show how they are both right. Snakes can be very scary, but they also can do some things like tasting the air that make them really cool.

Lead A or B? ____ Why? _____

_____

Share and Compare

With a partner, share and compare the leads you each selected. Did you make the same choices? Why or why not?

Your Turn

You have read a lead from a published author and have chosen a lead from two samples. Now it's time to do some creating of your own. Choose a topic from the following list, or make up a topic of your own.

- Your favorite reptile
- Baby animals
- An outdoor adventure
- A long car trip
- A different topic _____

You are going to write two leads. One of them should be a strong lead. Create a lead that will make your reader want to keep reading. The other lead needs to be weak. Make it so dull that your readers will want to run from your writing. It might help to look back at the examples you've just read to remind yourself how strong and weak leads sound.

Lead #1

_____

_____

_____

Lead #2

_____

_____

_____

Share

When you've finished writing, read your leads aloud with a partner. Can you tell which lead is your partner's strong lead? Can your partner pick out your strong lead?

A Writer's Question

Look at the lead in a book you've read recently. Is it strong or weak? Now that you know the whole story, what did the author say in the lead to pull you into the book?

Strong lead _____ Weak lead _____

How did the author use the lead to pull you into the story?

_____

_____

Lesson 6

name: .... date: ....

That's an Order!

How to Get Rich and Have a High-Seas Adventure

Directions: Start digging. Take a sea voyage to the island where the treasure is buried. Hire a crew to sail your ship. Find a treasure map in an old sailor's trunk. Ask someone with a large sailing ship whether you can borrow it. Hide your treasure in a safe spot. Beware of any one-legged seafaring men who sign on as your cook and cabin boy. Uncover the hidden treasure! Follow the map!

Did you notice anything wrong with this plan for getting rich quickly (besides sounding a lot like the plot of *Treasure Island*)? If you said that the directions seem out of order, give yourself a gold doubloon, matey. It would be difficult to start digging before you had a map. It would be awkward getting to the island before you found a ship or crew. When you write, putting information in order is important. Your words are a map for readers to follow. Their "treasure" is an understanding (and enjoyment) of your ideas. Leave them a clear, ordered, and interesting trail, and your readers will find the treasure every time.

Sharing an Example: The Greedy Triangle

The Greedy Triangle by Marilyn Burns is an amusing math story about a triangle who begins to wish for more in life— more sides and angles. As the triangle becomes too greedy, though, its life becomes complicated. Read the passage. You'll notice that the author's "map" has been changed a little. Is the map hard to follow? See whether you can follow along.

Poof! The shapeshifter turned the triangle into a quadrilateral.

"I think if I had just one more side and one more angle," said the triangle, "my life would be more interesting."

"How may I help you?" the shapeshifter asked the triangle.

So the triangle went to see the local shapeshifter.

"I'm tired of doing the same old things," it grumbled. "There must be more to life."

One day, the triangle began to feel dissatisfied.

"That's easy to do," said the shapeshifter.

Your Response

Were you able to follow the "map"? Does it make any sense at all? Write your response here.

_____ It makes NO sense! I am lost!

_____ I get the main idea, but that's about it.

_____ This is very easy to follow. I found the treasure!

Back on Track

Now read the original passage by Marilyn Burns. Is it an improvement over the version you just read? _____

One day, the triangle began to feel dissatisfied. "I'm tired of doing the same old things," it grumbled. "There must be more to life." So the triangle went to see the local shapeshifter.

"How may I help you?" the shapeshifter asked the triangle.

"I think if I had just one more side and one more angle," said the triangle, "my life would be more interesting."

"That's easy to do," said the shapeshifter. Poof! The shapeshifter turned the triangle into a quadrilateral.

Marilyn Burns. *The Greedy Triangle.* (New York: Scholastic, Inc., 1994) p. 1

Your Response

Did you see and hear a difference between the first passage and the second one? Was the second version easier to follow? Write your thoughts here.

_____

_____

_____

Cleaning Up the Map

The map for the following passage is definitely jumbled. Read the passage to get a feeling for what it is about. Then read it again carefully to see whether you can fix it by putting the eight sentences in order. Put a small number **1** before the sentence you think should go first, a number **2** before the sentence you think should go second, and so on. Put a number before every sentence.

The Great Cool-Off

___ The pool at Carl's house has a small water slide in the deep end. ___ Cameron has a big front lawn, perfect for water fights. ___ Later in the afternoon, when it got really hot, we could hike into the woods to our fort. ___ With a plan like this, we were ready to beat the heat. ___ Around the middle of the day, we could head to Carl's apartment for a swim. ___ There's so much shade around the fort that it never gets too hot. ___ I thought we could start the day with a water fight over at Cameron's house. ___ It was supposed to be 90 degrees out, so we would need a great plan to keep ourselves from melting.

Share and Compare

When you have finished numbering the eight sentences, compare results with a partner. Read your revised paragraphs aloud to each other. Can you follow each other's map of the paragraph? Did you decide on the same order as your partner? Is there more than one good way to organize this paragraph?

A Writer's Question

How organized is your own writing? Take a piece of your own writing (it can be a rough draft) and quietly read it aloud. Circle the number that shows how organized your writing is.

1	2	3	4	5	6
Really out of order!		Pretty organized— I think!			Super organized!

name: .... date: ....

Sticking with It

A writing idea spends a lot of time inside your head. While it's in there, you can shape it, add to it, chip away some unneeded parts, or even delete it if you want to. In your mind, that writing idea makes perfect sense, and all its pieces and parts seem clearly organized. Once you put the idea on paper, though, it becomes something else. What once seemed a clear pattern is now a jumble of topics, leaving your readers confused. Remember that readers cannot see inside your head. They see only what you have written on the paper. You need to think like a reader when you write.

What's the BIG Idea?

Here's a chance for you to be the reader and to ask whether this writer stuck to his or her main idea. Read the sample paragraph, "My Dad the Packer." When you finish reading, write what you think the main idea might be.

My Dad the Packer

In our family, getting off to a good start on a trip means following one simple rule: get your own suitcase ready to go, and set it down next to the car. If it is raining, put your bag in the garage. Usually the garage is crowded with bikes, tools, and stuff from projects we are all working on, which makes it hard to find a place to put anything. There's always a clear path to the freezer where we keep the ice cream, frozen jam, and homemade applesauce. We always make applesauce after getting apples from this farm. It is great stuff! If you don't want to make my dad mad, you remember never to put your bag inside the car unless my dad, the packer, tells you exactly where it's going to fit. He has this way of looking at all the bags, then looking at the car, and then walking back and forth, back and forth, until he suddenly shouts, "Yes!" He has a pretty loud voice, even when he talks on the phone. You should hear him cheer for our football team! Once he shouts, "Yes!" he moves nonstop until the car is packed. Then he circles the car, staring at his work with this grin on his face. He has a nice smile, and it has shown up in every picture we have ever taken of him. When he was younger, he had braces, and now his teeth are nearly perfect. I'll probably have to have braces in another couple of years. My dad is proud of his work.

Your Response

What do you think is the main idea of "My Dad the Packer"? Write your thoughts here.

_____

_____

_____

_____

_____

Did the Author Stick or Stray?

Writers can sometimes lose focus and wander off into other topics. Read "My Dad the Packer" again. This time draw a line through any parts where the writer has wandered from the main topic. Be careful not to cross out too much. Then read what is left of the paragraph to see whether it still makes sense.

Share and Compare

When you have finished, compare your paragraph with a partner's. Did each of you cross out the same parts? Did you agree on the main idea? If you did not, discuss and explain your differences.

Your Turn

It's your turn to be the writer. Think about what your family goes through to get ready for a trip or an outing. Are there rules about what to bring or who puts things in the car? Who gets to decide where everyone sits? How do you entertain yourselves in the car? List six to eight details that relate to preparing for a trip or an outing.

1. _____

2. _____

3. _____

4. _____

5. _____

6. _____

7. _____

8. _____

Now look at your list. Is every item a detail about getting ready for a family trip? Did you wander off topic as the writer of "My Dad the Packer" did? To keep yourself on topic, cross out any details that are not connected to your main topic.

When you are sure you have enough details to support your main topic, write a short paragraph about getting ready for a family trip. Make sure that all your details are connected to your topic. As you write, it's OK to add new details as long as you stay with your topic.

A Writer's Question

How would you rate your paragraph? Did you stay on topic? Read your paragraph to a partner to get his or her opinion.

____ **I stuck to the topic!**

____ **I wandered, but a reader could get the main idea.**

____ **I wandered off into the sunset and left readers scratching their heads.**

Lesson 8

Beware, the End Is Near!

Imagine a door at the end of a hallway. Above this door is a clearly marked EXIT sign. The end of a story, or conclusion, is like that hallway. If you're really enjoying yourself, you take your time moving down the hall. You know it's the way out. You know where you're headed and what's coming. When you reach the door, the handle turns easily. You are a bit sad to leave, but you know it is time.

Share an Example: The Wreckers

Here's an example from Ian Lawrence's *The Wreckers.* Read the passage, and see whether you feel yourself moving down the hallway. Do you sense the EXIT coming?

. . . I don't know what happened to Mary and Simon Mawgan. I don't know what became of the Widow.

But I do know this. The storms still thrash at the coast of Cornwall. The waves eat at the rock with a pounding of surf and spray. Never again will a sailor look up from a storm-tossed deck and see the false beacons gutter and burn. The wreckers only sit and wait. But on the darkest, wildest nights—or so the story goes—the corpse lights still walk on the beach on the Tombstones.

Ian Lawrence. *The Wreckers.* (New York: Bantam Doubleday Dell Books, 1998) p. 191

Your Response

What do you think of this conclusion? Does it sound as if the writer is wrapping up? (Did you see the EXIT sign approaching?)

_____

_____

_____

_____

_____

Select a Conclusion

Read the short passage called "Lost in the Storm" and the three possible conclusions for it. Decide which conclusion wraps up the story best (think of the EXIT at the end of the hallway), and circle the number of your choice.

Lost in the Storm

For once, the TV weather forecasters were right about something, or maybe they were just lucky in a weird sort of way. All I know is that they said the storm would come and that it would be bad. They were right. The wind started blowing the night before, just as they said it would, so school was canceled everywhere. I wasn't worried about the storm. I was just glad for a day off from school. All I was thinking about were the things I was going to do. Almost all of them involved my friends or my dog. And then the power went out, and it was dark. This was a thick dark, like a camping-in-the-woods-in-the-middle-of-nowhere dark. It freaked me out, so I called for my dog. Meeka would protect me, but where was she? I called her name several times. There was no answer. And then the sky lit up, as if our house were caught in the headlight of a train. Silence for a moment, and then BOOM! Thunder like a cannon rolled over our house, and all I could think of was the 4th of July, fireworks, and Meeka. Last summer she had run away at the first thudding sound of fireworks.

Possible Conclusions

1 At first I had wanted my dog to protect me. Now I wanted to protect my dog. I put on my raincoat and ran outside, ignoring the screams of my parents. I had to save my dog. Just when I thought I couldn't go any farther, I heard a bark, and then Meeka jumped into my arms.

2 Meeka was lost in the storm and I was worried. Then I heard a scratch at the door. It was Meeka, and I let her in. We were all safe now. The End.

3 My panic lasted for several minutes. The flashing and pounding of the thunder and lightning hammered at my head, and I couldn't think. I forced myself to stand and look outside, and then I remembered. When she had run away last summer, we had finally found her at the playground about a half a mile away. "The playground!" I shouted towards my mom. We both ran to the door. My mom wouldn't let me go alone, so she went with me. I don't really remember running to the playground, but we did. My mom held my hand the whole way, until I could see the play structure. In the little wooden house at the top of the slide was Meeka, shivering in a corner just as she had last summer. She wouldn't move, so my mom and I squeezed in and sat with her. It was cold and wet, but Meeka was safe.

What's Your Choice?

Which conclusion seems to do the best job of finishing the story?

I chose conclusion _____ because _____

_____ .

Your Hallway, Your EXIT, Your Turn

"Pieces of Eight" is about a girl who loves pirate stories and is positive that she has pirates in her family tree. Read the passage carefully and then create an ending for this story.

Pieces of Eight

Ann had read every pirate book and story in the school library. She was even teased about it by a group of boys who told her, "A girl can't be a pirate!" They stopped making fun when she showed them the book about Anne Bonney, a real woman pirate from the 1700s. When Ann read this book, she was convinced she was somehow related to Anne Bonney. She even began adding an "e" to the end of her name on all her school papers. Yes, she told herself, her name was the same as a pirate's, her grandparents had always lived on the coast, they didn't like talking about their family's past, and then there was one other tiny piece of evidence. Just last week she had found an old wooden box buried in the sand by the northeast corner of her grandparents' house.

Your conclusion: _____

_____

_____

_____

_____

_____

A Writer's Question

You know the importance of a good conclusion, but sometimes there are books that you wish would not end. Write the titles of two books that you didn't want to end. What did you like about these books?

Title 1 _____

Title 2 _____

Unit 3 Voice

Think about books you've read or listened to. When you read or hear a book you *really* like, the book probably has strong voice. Of course, just as no two people have the same personality, no two writers have the same voice. As you read and listen to various voices, you'll probably find yourself drawn more to some than to others. What you want—as a writer or reader—is writing that is strong in voice.

In this unit you'll learn about

◆ matching voice with purpose

◆ revising to make voice stronger

◆ imitating a favorite voice

◆ writing with a strong voice

name: .... date: ....

Matching Voice and Purpose

Imagine mowing the lawn with scissors and a comb or painting a house with a toothbrush and a dust mop. Imagine carrying your books to school with a cabbage leaf and rubber bands. In each of these cases, the tools don't match the size or the type of job. It would be much easier to start with the right tools in the first place. Writers are the same way about voice. They try to choose the right voice for the writing task.

Sharing an Example: Soldier's Heart

Here is an example from *Soldier's Heart,* a fictional story about a fifteen-year-old boy who becomes a soldier in the Civil War. Read the passage. Notice the author's voice as he introduces his main character, Charley, and the reason Charley so desperately wants to become a soldier.

There would be a shooting war. There were rebels who had violated the law and fired on Fort Sumter and the only thing they'd respect was steel, it was said, and he knew they were right, and the Union was right, and one other thing they said as well—if a man didn't hurry he'd miss it. The only shooting war to come in a man's life and if a man didn't step right along he'd miss the whole thing.

Charley didn't figure to miss it. The only problem was that Charley wasn't rightly a man yet, at least not to the army. He was fifteen and while he worked as a man worked, in the fields all of a day and into night, and looked like a man standing tall and just a bit thin with hands so big they covered a stove lid, he didn't make a beard yet and his voice had only just dropped enough so he could talk with men.

If they knew, he thought, if they knew he was but fifteen they wouldn't take him at all.

But Charley watched and Charley listened and Charley learned.

Gary Paulsen. *Soldier's Heart.* (New York: Delacorte Press, 1998) pp. 2–3

Voice and Purpose

How would you describe the author's voice? Circle each word that matches what you think (you can circle more than one).

serious   sad   humorous   angry   tense   quiet

How did the voice you heard match what you expected from a book on the Civil War?

_____ totally different   _____ exact match   _____ a mix of both

The Reason for Writing: Using Voice As a Clue

Sometimes the voice a writer uses helps explain why the writer is writing. Read Sample 1 carefully. Then, list some descriptive words that tell about the voice the writer used. See whether the voice suggests a clue about the writer's purpose.

Sample 1

Far below the earth's surface, water drips from the roof of a cave. The drops fall through the darkness into a large stone room no one has ever seen. No bird has ever sung here. The scent of wildflowers has never hung in the air. For thousands of years, the tomblike silence has been broken only by the sound of falling water. Drip. Drip. Drip.

Stephen Kramer. *Caves.* (Minneapolis: Carolrhoda Books, Inc., 1995) p. 1

What words best describe this voice? Write them here.

_____

_____

_____

What is the writer's purpose? Check one.

_____ to make us laugh

_____ to teach us about caves

_____ to scare us

On-Key or Off-Key Voice?

When the voice does not match the purpose, the writing can sound a little off—like a singer hitting the wrong note. Read the following business letter to Ace Plumbing to see whether you think the writer has done a good job of matching voice and purpose.

Dear Ace Plumbing:

Those were super-terrific new pipes you installed under my sink! Wow! Plus the plumber worked so fast, he was like lightening! He was barely here—then he was gone. Good grief! I can't get over how super-efficient and amazing your great little company is! You will get all my plumbing business for the next quadrillion years!

Your Response

What do you think of the voice in the letter to Ace Plumbing?

_____ The voice is perfect for a business letter.

_____ OK, but the voice could use more energy.

_____ This letter has voice, but it's not the right voice for this job.

Write any thoughts or reasons you have here.

A Writer's Question

Find a piece of your own writing. How would you describe the voice? Do you think the voice is a good match for the purpose of the writing?

_____

_____

_____

name: .... date: ....

Raising Your Voice

One of the best ways to express your writing voice is to write about what you know. Telling your stories and sharing your experiences are what personal narrative writing is all about. When you write about your life, every word *is* you—what you have seen, what you have done, whom you have known, where you have been, and how you have felt. If you hold back or settle for vague descriptions, your readers won't understand or appreciate your experience. Bring your stories to life by filling every word with the energy of the moment. Your readers will be energized as well, and they will feel as if they're right there, sharing the moment with you.

Rank the Voice

Here are three short samples of personal narrative writing. The writers are telling you about their lives and experiences. Read each sample, looking and listening for its voice. Then, rank each sample according to the strength of voice.

Sample A

The Climbing Wall

I have climbed mountains. I have scrambled across the rugged slopes of tall peaks. I have clung to the side of a cliff with nothing to hold me but my hands and feet. Where have I done these daring deeds? Mt. Everest? No, all this happened on the climbing wall in the gym at my school. OK, so I exaggerated a little, but when it's my turn to go across the wall, I let my imagination go. Instead of cushy, padded mats on the floor, I see jagged rocks below. The climber behind me is a shaggy mountain goat, and the person in front is a photographer from National Geographic. My teacher always says I look exhausted when I get back from PE, and I just smile.

Sample B

Fireworks

I love fireworks, don't you? I like the colors, the sounds, and the bright flashes of light. They are so pretty and scary at the same time. On the Fourth of July, I always go somewhere to watch fireworks. There should be fireworks at every holiday. Fireworks are the best.

Sample C

Picking Blackberries

Every summer I go with my dad to pick blackberries. We have a secret spot that we go to on the edge of this lake near our house. We act like spies on a top-secret mission as we hike quietly to the blackberry patch.

If you have ever picked them before, you know how sharp the barbs on the vines can be. We wear long-sleeved shirts and long pants to protect our arms and legs, even when it's hot. My dad calls the vines the barbed wire that surrounds the enemy base we are breaking into. We always have fun, and the jam we make is good, too.

Voice Rankings

Think about the amount of voice in each sample as you write your rankings here. Put the title of each narrative in the blank where it fits best.

1. _____ (strong voice, great energy)

2. _____ (so-so voice, medium energy)

3. _____ (weak voice, low energy)

Talk About the Voices

Get ready to share your voice rankings with the rest of your class. How do they compare? Be prepared to discuss any differences of opinion. Remember that discussing involves talking *and* listening. Someone else's ideas may help you understand voice.

From a Whisper to a Shout!

The narratives that you ranked 2 and 3 need help developing voice. Their voices are whispering when they need to be shouting! Choose one of the passages you ranked weaker in voice. Then revise it to make the voice stronger. Look for moments when you think the author needs help creating strong voice. Raise the voice from a whisper to a shout by adding some details or changing any words that will help the reader share the writer's experience.

Sample _____ with my revisions:

_____

_____

_____

_____

_____

_____

_____

Share and Compare

When you have finished revising, share your changes with a partner. Did you both make the same kinds of revisions? What revisions did each of you make to strengthen the voice?

A Writer's Question

What advice would you give another writer who wanted help in strengthening the voice in a personal narrative? Write your advice here.

Dear Writer,

_____

_____

_____

_____

_____

name: .... date: ....

All-star Voices

As you walk down the aisles of your favorite library or bookstore, the great voices that live in books practically call out to you. Some are old friends, and some are new ones. These memorable voices can be funny or sad, scary or silly, relaxed or serious. Sharing favorite voices and books is one way to help someone hear a new voice and perhaps to find a new favorite book. By listening to new and different voices, you might find a voice that you'd like to use in your own writing.

Sharing an Example: Silent to the Bone

Here is an example of voice from E.L. Konigsburg. In her book, thirteen-year-old Connor tries to help his friend Branwell, who has not spoken since his little sister was injured in a terrible accident.

When Branwell rides his bike, he gets his pants leg caught in the chain of his bicycle. When he sits next to you in the bleachers, he sits too close. When he laughs at one of your jokes, he laughs too loud. When he eats a peanut butter and jelly sandwich, he ends up with a pound of peanut butter caught in his braces.

When he sits too close, I tell him to back off. When he has peanut butter stuck in his braces, I tell him to clean it up. When he gets his pants leg caught in his bicycle chain, I stop and wait for him to get untangled.

I figure that Branwell got his awkwardness from his father, and I guess I got my acceptance from my mother. And here's the final thing I have to say about being friends with Branwell. He is different, but no one messes with him because everyone knows there is a lot to Branwell besides the sitting-too-close and the laughing-too-loud. They just don't choose to be his friend. But I do. Who else would invite a guy over to hear his new CD of Mozart's Prague Symphony and let him listen without having to pretend that he likes it or pretend that he doesn't? Who else would ask a question like "If a tree falls in the forest and no one is there to hear it, does it make a sound?" the first thing in the morning?

E.L. Konigsburg. *Silent to the Bone.* (New York: Atheneum Books for Young Readers, 2000) pp. 18–19

Listen and Learn

Be prepared to talk about this passage with your class. What kind of voice did you hear? How did it make you feel? What does Connor's voice tell you about him? What does his voice tell you about his friendship with Branwell? Write some notes about the author's voice.

_____

_____

_____

An All-Star Voice

Think about books *you* have read that you liked and remember well. Those books probably have strong voice. Choose a favorite book to share with the class. Skim through it to find a part with powerful voice. To make sure the part is the one you want and that it's long enough to let the voice come through, read it aloud to yourself. You may want to do this several times, so that you will feel confident sharing it.

Title: _____

Author: _____

Pages I want to share: _____

The reason I chose this book: _____

_____

_____

Trying Another Voice

For a young writer, it's important not only to find and hear new voices, but also to imitate them as a way of practicing. You will try imitating voice by selecting one of the author's voices you heard in your sharing group. You may choose the voice that you shared or the voice that another group member shared. You may also choose the voice in the passage from *Silent to the Bone.* After you have made your choice, write a short paragraph using a voice as *much like that writer's voice as you can.*

Choose your own topic, and try to make your paragraph sound as though the author you selected had written it. For example, Connor's voice in *Silent to the Bone* is honest and straightforward. He doesn't make excuses for his friend; he just describes Branwell as he is. You could imitate that voice by writing about something in a similarly honest way. Remember that you are imitating an author's voice, not copying the words.

name: .... date: ....

_____

_____

_____

_____

_____

_____

_____

_____

_____

_____

_____

A Writer's Question

What kind of voice did you choose to imitate? What is the greatest difference between your own writing voice and the voice you imitated?

name: .... date: ....

It's All About You

If your teacher asked everyone in your class to write about a favorite holiday, you might think that all the writing would be much the same. Holidays are holidays, right? But did everyone have exactly the same thing to eat? Did everyone drop the dessert down the stairs by accident? People are individuals with their own stories and special moments. When you write, you want to include the details that show how your special moments are different from everyone else's. That difference is part of what gives your writing voice.

Setting the Channel to MSV

To get started, read the list of suggested topics. You may choose any of these or decide on a topic of your own. When you choose a writing topic you know and care about, your voice will come through strong and clear. Your job in this lesson is to write a short paragraph, six or more sentences, with the channel set to MSV—My Strong Voice.

My favorite holiday moment

The best kind of day to be me

I felt annoyed

It happened in my backyard

A nighttime adventure

A different idea _____

A Little Push

Use any prewriting strategy you know to help you focus on a topic. You can use an idea web, a word collection, a list of questions, a drawing, or anything else that helps. Use this space for your prewriting.

Write! Write! Write!

Use your prewriting ideas to help you start writing. The focus of this lesson is writing with voice, so set your voice free. Remember to add those details that show how your experience (what you saw, what you felt) was *different* from everyone else's. Let your readers see what you saw and feel what you felt. Turn readers into participants, not just spectators.

_____

_____

_____

_____

_____

_____

_____

_____

_____

_____

_____

_____

_____

_____

_____

Rest and Reflect

When you have finished writing your paragraph, read it aloud to yourself. Do more than look at the words and sentences. Really listen! How would you describe your voice in the short piece you just wrote? Describe the voice here as clearly as possible.

I would describe my voice as

_____

_____

You Be the Judge

Now you need to try thinking about your voice from a different angle. Use the scale to rate the strength and energy of your writing voice. Whether your voice is quiet or loud, silly or serious, it needs to have its own energy. Think back to the passage from *Silent to the Bone.* The author's voice was quiet, honest, and energized, as Connor revealed how well he understood his friend Branwell. How strong is your voice? How energized is it? Rate it here.

1	**2**	**3**	**4**	**5**	**6**

Small voice, I'm holding back— energy on low.

Very strong voice, super-charged and powerful. No holding back!

A Writer's Question

Before today, you looked and listened for voice in other people's writing. You saw examples of strong and weak voice written by someone other than yourself. In today's lesson, the focus was on your writing and your voice. What is one important thing you learned about *your* voice today?

Unit 4
Word Choice

Think of the last time you read something that was either hard to understand or very boring. Chances are that the source of the problem was a writer's poor choice of words. Words are like gifts from a writer to a reader. A writer should choose words with the same care he or she would put into choosing a gift.

In this unit, you will create a wonderful gift by learning about

◆ choosing strong verbs

◆ using context to determine word meaning

◆ "painting pictures" with sensory language

◆ cutting out clutter

name: .... date: ....

Lights, Camera, Action!

On a movie set, a director can always yell, "Cut!" if he or she does not like the way an actor reads a line. After fixing the problem, the director can restart the scene by shouting, "Action!" As a writer, you get to be the director of your writing. You get to choose every word you put on the paper, and choosing the best words is especially important. Strong, descriptive verbs give writing energy, which really brings out the writer's voice as well. If your writing doesn't have the energy it needs, "Cut!" the weak words and yell, "Action!" to bring on the verbs.

Sharing an Example: A Year Down Yonder

In the Newbery award-winning novel *A Year Down Yonder,* Mary Alice is spending a year in her Grandma Dowdel's small town. Grandma Dowdel, always unpredictable, decides to use a tractor that doesn't belong to her for a pecan-picking adventure. Read the passage on page 60. Notice how the writer/director, Richard Peck, energizes his writing with strong action words, the words in color.

I was transfixed. I couldn't think a moment ahead. Now she was half swallowed by the darkness of the barn door. Then she was swallowed.

I stood like a sculpture in the yard. An ear-splitting explosion rocked the night. The tractor roared to life, coughing and gunning. Old Man Nyquist's dog shot out from under the porch, yelping, and chased himself all over the yard. The tractor lurched forward, gathering speed. As it crossed the moonlit yard, there was Grandma up in the tractor seat, white-headed and high. She could start it, but could she stop it?

The pecan tree stopped it.

Grandma, who didn't know how to drive an automobile, aimed at the tree and hit it dead on, ramming it with the tire over the radiator. The tree reeled in shock, and pecans rained. It was a good thing I wasn't standing under it. A ton of pecans fell together, like a hailstorm. When the tractor hit bark, it bounced back and the engine died. Grandma's head snapped back, but she was still riding it. Now she was climbing down.

Richard Peck, *A Year Down Yonder* (New York: Dial Books for Young Readers, 2000), p. 31

Writing Without the Action Words

From the energy of the strong action words (verbs), were you able to see and feel what was happening to Mary Alice and Grandma Dowdel? Do you think the writing would have worked as well if the author had used weaker action words? To find out, read this second version in which all the strong action words have been replaced with weaker choices.

I was standing still. I couldn't think a moment ahead. Now she was half hidden by the darkness of the barn door. Then she was hidden.

I stood like a sculpture in the yard. An ear-splitting explosion made noise in the night. The tractor came to life, running and turning. Old Man Nyquist's dog ran out from under the porch, barking, and ran himself all over the yard. The tractor moved forward, adding speed. As it moved over the moonlit yard, there was Grandma up in the tractor seat, white-headed and high. She could start it, but could she stop it?

The pecan tree stopped it.

Grandma, who didn't know how to drive an automobile, moved toward the tree and hit it dead on, touching it with the tire over the radiator. The tree moved in shock, and pecans fell. It was a good thing I wasn't standing under it. A ton of pecans fell together, like a hailstorm. When the tractor hit bark, it came back and the engine stopped. Grandma's head moved back, but she was still riding it. Now she was getting down.

Your Response

What did you think about the *second* version?

_____ The words were *much* stronger.

_____ I couldn't see much difference.

_____ It was very dull. There was no action!

Spotting the Action Words

Read the next passage. Underline any verbs that are strong and powerful enough to be action words.

Run for Cover

When the rain started, hardly anyone noticed. The parents on the sidelines had their eyes locked on their kids out in the field. The kids meanwhile were busy scrambling for position, dodging around one another or trying to blast the ball into the net. The first raindrops fell silently, cushioned by the grass and deflected by the moving players. Then, suddenly, the clouds ripped open and rain streamed down. Giant drops slammed onto everyone as parents hustled to grab chairs, cameras, and kids, and dash for cover. The players on the field were the last to notice. Several of them gazed up at the dark sky with their mouths gaping open. Heavy drops pounded their faces and mouths and they found themselves spitting and gulping what didn't bounce off. Then, as suddenly as it had started, the rain stopped.

Share and Compare

With a partner, share your underlined verbs. Did both of you underline the same action words?

Directing Your Own Writing

The next step is to practice putting strong action words into your own writing. Choose a topic from the list or come up with an idea of your own. Write a paragraph with at least six sentences. Concentrate on choosing strong verbs that will energize your idea. Remember that you are the director of this paragraph. If you are not happy with what you write the first time, cut what you wrote and choose another way to say it. Ready? Action!

- An experience at a sporting event
- Putting up with bad weather
- Playing on a rainy, cold day
- Trying something new to eat
- A different idea _____

_____

_____

_____

_____

_____

_____

A Writer's Question

What is the best thing about being the "director" of everything you write? What is the hardest part?

Headline News— use Writer's clues!

name: .... date: ....

As a writer, you are in charge of every word that goes into your writing. The "word bank" of words you can choose from grows larger as you read books, newspapers, magazines—even the cereal box on the breakfast table. Suppose you come across a great new word such as *conveyance.* You'd like to add it to your bank, but you're not sure what the word means. Try looking at the context: the way the word is used in a sentence or paragraph: "He had to walk because his only means of *conveyance,* his bike, had a flat tire." Can you guess what *conveyance* means by looking at how it's used in this sentence? If you guessed *a form of transportation,* you were right! *Conveyance* can now go into your vocabulary bank. This lesson shows you how to make use of context clues every time you read.

Desert Island Words: The Thief

Look at the list of words on page 64. These words are stranded on a desert island without any other words or sentences to keep them company. It's harder to figure out the meaning of each word without the help of other words, but give it a try. Read the list with a partner. Think about and discuss what each word *might* mean. Make your best guess, and write it in the column called Possible Meanings. Remember that words often have more than one meaning.

	Possible Meanings	Meaning from Context
1. twilight		
2. ravine		
3. reliably		
4. granite		
5. magus		
6. inquiries		
7. succession		
8. descend		
9. converted		
10. basilica		
11. pantheon		
12. deity		

Putting Words Back in Context

Now the words on the list will be put back into the sentences they came from—they will go back in **context.** These words were taken from a passage in a book called *The Thief.* Gen, the thief of the title, is a boy whose "skill" lands him in prison and then on a mission to find an ancient treasure. The words from the list are in color so that you can find them easily. As you read the passage, use the context of each sentence to help you figure out the meaning of each word. With your partner, write what you think the meaning of each word *might* be in the column marked Meaning from Context.

Twilight came mercifully early in the deep ravine of the streambed. Our party slowed down once we could no longer see to place our feet reliably. Pol helped me along, and I had to take a hand from Ambiades as well. Finally we came to a wider area of the trail and a flat space that had served many travelers as a camping spot. Someone had built a stone fireplace against the wall of the ravine, and the granite above it was blackened by many fires.

After dinner, when our bedrolls were spread out on the ground behind us, we sat around the fire, and Ambiades asked again why we were in Eddis. The magus answered with another question, which Ambiades answered patiently, obviously used to this response to his inquiries.

"What do you know about the rule of succession in Eddis?"

"Well, they have a queen, like Attolia, so the throne can't descend only in the male line. I suppose the rule is passed from parent to child, just like Sounis."

"And do you know if that has always been true?"

Ambiades shrugged. "Since the invaders."

"And before?"

"Are you talking about Hamiathes's Gift?" Ambiades caught on quickly.

"I am," said the magus, and turned to Sophos. "Do you know about the Gift?" Sophos didn't, so the magus explained.

"It's not surprising. Sounis and Attolia long ago converted to the invader's religion, and we worship those gods in the basilica in the city, but once we all worshipped the gods of the mountain country. There is an almost infinite pantheon with a deity for each spring and river, mountain and forest, but there is a higher court of more powerful gods ruled by Hephestia, goddess of fire and lightning. She governs all the gods except her mother, the Earth, and her father, the Sky."

Megan Whelen Turner, *The Thief* (New York: Penguin Group, 1996), pp. 54–55

Discuss and Check

Now it's time to discuss with your partner what you think each word means. Be as specific as possible about the context clues you used to help shape your guesses. After you discuss the word meanings with your partner, check the definitions in a dictionary.

A Writer's Question

Being willing to add new words to your vocabulary will help keep your writing interesting and fresh. How many of the words on the list were new to you? Choose three words from the list and try to use them in a conversation before the end of the day. For example, you might say, "What method of conveyance will you use to go home today?"

Number of words new to you _____

Words you will use in a conversation _____

_____

_____

Lesson 15

Painting Word Pictures

When you begin to write, think of yourself as a word artist. A painter chooses the subject, the style, the colors—everything! A writer chooses everything as well: the topic, the voice, the style, and of course, every word. Think of each word as a brush stroke of color or light. If the writer has chosen the right words, including sensory words, the resulting picture will be clear, strong, and inviting.

Sharing an Example: Homeless Bird

Sensory words are words that connect to the *senses* of sight, hearing, touch, smell, and taste. Here is an example of sensory language used in a passage from the book *Homeless Bird*. The book tells the story of thirteen-year-old Koly and her life in India, including the problems she faces from an arranged marriage. She actually enjoys her trips to the river to wash clothes because she gets a chance to be out in nature. Read the passage. Look *and* listen for the sensory words that paint a picture in your mind.

I looked forward to those walks to the river, for I was walking away from Sass and her scolding. It was June and hot summer now. Along the road I saw women winnowing baskets of threshed grain in the wind, the clouds of chaff flying off in the breeze. The mustard fields were golden with blossoms and smelled fragrant when I walked by them. In this dry season only a trickle of muddy water remained in the river. Though I rubbed the clothes on the stones to get them clean, the clothes sometimes looked even dirtier when I was finished.

Still, I loved the river. Sometimes a tiny silver fish would leap from the water after a fly. Hawks circled overhead. Bright-green dragonflies wove in and out of the reeds. A kingfisher perched on a people tree, its red breast like a tongue of fire. I washed the dust off my bare feet and splashed the water over me for the coolness. I thought of how Hari had splashed me in the Ganges. I wondered what my life would have been like as Hari's wife. I knew that Hari had been spoiled and would not have been easy to live with, yet I was sure I would have been happier than I was now.

Gloria Whelan, *Homeless Bird* (New York: HarperCollins Children's Books, 2000), pp. 68–69

Sensory Reaction

Look carefully at the passage once again. Underline any sensory details, and then compare findings with your partner. Did you underline the same words? Notice how the details are organized in the table below.

I see	I hear	I feel	I smell	I taste
clouds of chaff	scolding	hot summer	fragrant blossoms	
golden mustard blossoms	trickle of muddy water	dust on bare feet		
tiny silver fish	splash of water	cool water		
bright-green dragonflies				
kingfisher's red breast				

Your Own Table

Read the poem on page 69 about going to a baseball game. Underline examples of sensory language. Then list each example on the table that follows.

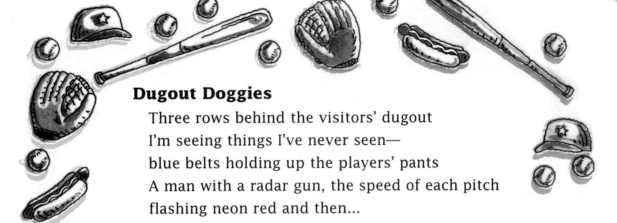

Dugout Doggies

Three rows behind the visitors' dugout
I'm seeing things I've never seen—
blue belts holding up the players' pants
A man with a radar gun, the speed of each pitch
flashing neon red and then...

First I smell them, spicy Polish sausage dogs,
hot brown mustard, and yes, one more sniff,
tangy sauerkraut!

Then I hear him calling, "Doggies! Dugout Doggies!
Get 'em while they're hot! Dugout Doggies!"
These aren't the hot dogs you get up in the nosebleed
cheapo bleacher seats.

Then I see him, red-and-white striped shirt,
through the steam rising off the glorious dogs,
holding a bag of buns
that suddenly leaps from his hands,
turning over and over and over and then down
softly into ready hands.
I stand and clap and cry, "Doggies, Dugout Doggies!
I need two!"
Three rows behind the visitors' dugout—life is *good*.

I see	I hear	I feel	I smell	I taste

Your Turn—Be a Word Artist

Picture yourself in one of these spots: a stadium (or other location) or out in nature, enjoying the beauty. Ask yourself what you can *see, hear, taste, touch,* or *smell.* As a way of prewriting, make some notes here:

I see _____

I hear _____

I taste _____

I touch _____

I smell _____

Now use your sensory detail notes to write a paragraph or short poem with at least six sentences. If you choose to write a poem, remember that it doesn't have to rhyme.

_____

_____

_____

_____

_____

_____

_____

A Writer's Question

Of the five senses—seeing, hearing, tasting, touching, and smelling—which is your *favorite* to include in the sensory language in your own writing? Which is the easiest to include? Which is the hardest?

name: .... date: ....

Brush Strokes, Not Buckets!

Pump too much air into your bike tire, and it just might explode. Add too much soap to your load of wash, and you'll end up with a flood of bubbles. Put too many words in a piece of writing, and you will risk confusing (and possibly losing) your readers. As a writer, you're trying to paint clear pictures in readers' minds. Overwhelming them with extra words is like trying to paint a picture of a delicate flower by hurling buckets of paint at the canvas. When you write, make every word count.

Sharing an Example: J.J. and Me: Friends or Twins?

Here's an example of writing that is too wordy. The unnecessary words—the clutter—may prevent the reader from understanding the main idea. Read the passage. See what you think: brush strokes or buckets?

Just across the street, on the other side of the road, is the house where my best friend lives. My best friend's name is J.J. His real name is John James, but everyone calls him by his nickname, J.J., for short. J.J. has lived in the house across the street for as long as I can remember. We're both eleven, and we've lived in this neighborhood and been best friends all of our lives. You wouldn't believe how similar our lives are in many of the same ways. It's somewhat like we're almost brothers but living in houses across the street from each other. J.J. has a brown Jack Russell terrier dog. I also have the exact same kind of dog, Jack Russell terrier. My dog is the same color as his except for one spot on the top of his head that is white instead of brown. We both have two sisters, and in each case, one sister is older and one sister is younger than we are. Our mothers' first names each begin with a "D." Pretty unbelievable, isn't it? Now you might be thinking to yourself that what I'm saying sounds like it can't be true, that it's all made up, that it's just a story. Well, everything I've said is true. You know what they say: Sometimes truth is stranger than fiction.

Your Response

How did this writing look and sound to you? Brush strokes or buckets?

_____ a little on the wordy side

_____ just about right

_____ WAY too wordy

Now, read through it again with a partner. Cross out any unnecessary words or sentences.

Side by Side

Now read a revised version of the paragraph. Compare it to your revision. Did you and your partner cut the same clutter?

J.J. and Me: Friends or Twins?

Just across the street is the house where my best friend John James lives. Everyone calls him J.J. We're both eleven, and we've lived in this neighborhood all our lives. You won't believe how similar our lives are. It's almost like we're brothers. J.J. and I have identical Jack Russell terriers, except my dog has a white spot on his head. We both have an older sister and a younger sister. Our mothers' first names each begin with a "D." It's pretty unbelievable, but I guess sometimes truth really is stranger than fiction.

Compare

Which of these statements do you think is true about the two revisions?

_____ My partner and I cut out even more clutter!

_____ My partner and I cut out about the same amount of clutter.

_____ My partner and I did not cut out all the clutter, but we still like our version.

_____ My partner and I did not cut out as much, but next time we would definitely cut out more!

Cut the Clutter

Here's another passage that needs careful brush strokes to remove the clutter. As you read through it, cross out any unnecessary parts. When you finish, use the writing space to rewrite the paragraph in its revised form. Make every word count! (**Tip:** You can change the punctuation or use different words if you wish.)

I like to spend a certain part of the day, at least a couple of hours, each weekend on Saturday or Sunday, in-line skating down by the river. There's a path that runs alongside one side of the Chippewa River that runs through town. The path along the river is for people who want to in-line skate, jog, walk, or even ride a bike. It's a place for all kinds of multiple uses for people with different interests. The only catch is that if you want to ride a bike or skate, you have to pay $10 for a year or $3 for a single one-day pass. There is no fee for walking or jogging; they're free. You don't have to pay if you are under 16, but if you are over 16, you have to pay. I'm under 16, so I don't have to pay a fee. The trail is paved for seven miles, and it's flat, not steep, so it's good for in-line skating because it's not too steep. It's a fun place to go on weekends or weekdays to do fun outdoor activities you like to do and enjoy doing.

_____

_____

_____

_____

_____

_____

_____

_____

Share and Compare

Meet with your partner to share your revision. What kinds of clutter did each of you cut? What other changes did each of you make? Discuss how you decided what clutter to remove.

A Writer's Question

What is the best way to explain clutter to a writer who needs to know what it is and how to spot it?

Sentence Fluency

Fluent writing is smooth and rhythmic. It is a pleasure to read, whether silently or aloud. As a writer, you want to develop fluency, but to do so, you must understand what makes writing fluent. The following lessons will help you learn the techniques that will help you become a more fluent writer.

In this unit you'll learn strategies to make your sentences more fluent and natural. You'll learn about

◆ combining sentences for fluency

◆ varying the length of sentences

◆ using dialogue

◆ revising for fluency

name: .... date: ....

Rolling Like a River

Like a calm river, fluent writing moves smoothly and steadily. It flows along easily, conveying ideas and images from writer to reader. Well-chosen words become rhythmic sentences that build to thoughtful paragraphs, each one clearly connected to the one before it.

Choppy sentences can interrupt the rhythmic ease of fluent writing. Sentences may start, stop, or change direction too often, becoming difficult to follow. To test the fluency of your writing, read it aloud. If your writing does not flow smoothly, it may need revision.

Sharing an Example: Sand Dune Adventure

Read the following example. As you read, ask yourself, "Does this flow as smoothly as a river? If not, why?"

I like to hike on the sand dunes. I like to hike to the very top. The hike can be difficult. There isn't really a trail. You have to zigzag back and forth. Your feet slip in the sand. Sometimes you have to crawl. I think it's easier without shoes. It's worse on sunny days. The sun really heats up the sand. The hot sand can burn your feet. Getting to the top has its rewards. The view is fantastic. You can see the ocean. You can see the mountains. You can see the river. You are king of the hill! There is something even better. The best part is going back down. It is fast. Running is the best way to go down. It is a thrill. It makes the climb worth the effort.

Your Response

How did this paragraph look and sound to you?

_____ It is full of starts and stops—no flow!

_____ It looks and sounds OK to me.

_____ It is very fluent and smooth.

Can You Find the Problem?

How did you rate "Sand Dune Adventure"? What problems does it have? Look at this list of possible problems, and put a check by any that describe "Sand Dune Adventure."

_____ The sentences are far too long.

_____ The sentences sound short and choppy.

_____ The writer tries to put too much information into each sentence.

_____ The writer does not put enough information into each sentence.

Revised Example: Sand Dune Adventure

It's likely that you said the sentences were too short and that they didn't have enough information. One way to fix writing like this is to combine sentences to improve the rhythm and flow. Read the revised version of "Sand Dune Adventure." Notice the sentences that have been combined.

I like to hike to the very top of the sand dunes. The hike can be difficult because there isn't really a trail. You have to zigzag back and forth, your feet slip in the sand, and sometimes you have to crawl. I think it's easier without shoes, except on sunny days. The sand can really heat up, and your feet can burn. Getting to the top is rewarding, though, because of the fantastic view of the ocean, the mountains, and river. You are king of the hill! The best part is running back down. It is so fast and thrilling that it makes the climb worth the effort.

Combining: How to Do It

Combining sentences is a great way to increase sentence fluency. When you're combining sentences, imagine that you are doing an addition problem in math. Here's how it worked with two sentences from "Sand Dune Adventure":

  I like to hike on the sand dunes.

+ I like to hike to the very top.

= I like to hike to the very top of the sand dunes.

Let's Get Rolling!

As you read the passage on page 79, think about which sentences you could "add" together to create a smoother flow.

The Giving Garden

My school has a garden. It is called The Giving Garden. Student volunteers and their families help take care of it. The volunteers help with the weeding and watering. The garden has some flowers. It is mainly a vegetable garden. Last year we grew potatoes. In September, we harvested the potatoes. There were almost four hundred pounds of potatoes. We gave the potatoes to a local food bank. There was a Harvest assembly. We weighed the potatoes at the assembly. We thanked all the volunteers. The school gave each of them a flower.

Revise

Read "The Giving Garden" one more time—with a pencil in your hand. Put a plus sign (+) between the sentences you think should be combined. Then write your revised version of "The Giving Garden."

_____

_____

_____

_____

_____

A Writer's Question

How did you do? Write the most fluent sentence you created by sentence combining.

My most fluent sentence: _____

_____

_____

name: .... date: ....

VARY Length— or Be VERY Boring!

What happens to fluency when all the sentences are about the same length? Let's see.

I like my dog. My dog is brown. Her name is Heidi. She can run fast. She likes to chew socks. Her fur is soft.

Writing like this is choppy and repetitive—and dull. Such flat monotony discourages readers. Use your revision skills—sentence combining, adding or eliminating details, or changing the beginning of sentences—to help improve the flow. Your writing will be much more fluent, imaginative, and appealing to readers.

Sharing an Example: The View from Saturday

Read this short passage from *The View from Saturday*. Look carefully at the flow and rhythm of the words and ideas. Pay close attention to sentence length.

Mrs. Olinski's very first teaching job had been in an elementary school whose principal required sixth graders to memorize at least fourteen lines of poetry each month, insisted that fifth graders know their multiplication tables up through twelve times twelve, and permitted no one to exchange valentines unless the names on the envelopes were written neatly and spelled correctly.

There was no graffiti on the walls; no gum chewing, running, or shoving in the halls. There was locker inspection once a month, and everyone who used the bathroom flushed.

That principal's name was Margaret Draper.

E.L. Konigsburg. *The View from Saturday.* (New York: Aladdin Paperbacks, 1996) p. 58

Your Response

What do you think of the fluency of this passage? How is it affected by the length of each sentence?

_____ It is not fluent—no variety in sentence length.

_____ Sentence fluency is OK—some variety in sentence length.

_____ It is very fluent—lots of variety in sentence length!

Check the Numbers

How did you rate this passage? Did you find this piece fluent, with plenty of variety in sentence length? Let's check by counting the words.

Number of sentences in passage: **4**

Number of words in each sentence:

Sentence 1	**59 words**
Sentence 2	**16 words**
Sentence 3	**14 words**
Sentence 4	**6 words**

The first sentence of the passage is rather long, but it works well. The author makes the principal's requirements seem overwhelming by putting them all together in one long sentence. The author finishes the description with a short sentence that has only one detail, the principal's name. This short sentence has the effect of an exclamation point, ending the description crisply and forcefully.

Your Turn to VARY Sentences

This next piece of writing needs help. As you read, think about how the fluency is affected by the number of words in each sentence.

Getting ready to travel is easy. First of all, choose your luggage. Ask, "How long is my trip?" Now, list the things you need. Check off what you already have. Circle anything you still need. When you have everything, begin packing. Put small items in separate bags. Roll big items to save space. Don't cram too much into one bag. Ask, "What can I live without?" Now, you are ready to go.

Do the Numbers

How did this passage sound? Smooth and flowing or choppy and repetitive? Before you decide, do the numbers. Count the number of words in each sentence. (There are 12 sentences.) Put each total in its own space. The first two have been done for you.

Number of words in each sentence:

<u>6</u> <u>6</u> __ __ __ __ __ __ __ __ __ __

What do you notice about these totals? What can you do to improve the fluency of this writing? Here's a list of revision strategies you may have practiced before:

1. Combine sentences that could go together. Change the punctuation if necessary.

2. Add any important details.

3. Delete any unnecessary information.

4. Try different sentence beginnings.

5. Emphasize an important point in a short, punchy sentence.

Time to Revise: Vary the Length

Reread the passage about packing, and use the list
of strategies to help you revise for sentence fluency.
(Hint: Leave the first sentence alone. It can be your
topic sentence!)

_____

_____

_____

_____

_____

_____

_____

_____

_____

_____

A Writer's Question

**Do the numbers on your revised
paragraph. Did your revised paragraph
have fewer sentences than the original?
Did you vary the sentence lengths to make
the writing more fluent? Circle the total for
your longest sentence, and put a box around
the total for your shortest sentence. What is
the difference between the two?**

**Number of sentences in revised paragraph: ____ (12 sentences
before revision)**

**Number of words in each sentence: ___ ___ ___ ___ ___
___ ___ ___ ___ ___ ___ (Mostly 6-word sentences
before revision)**

name: .... date: ....

Dynamite Dialogue

A conversation between characters in a story is called dialogue. An author uses dialogue to help readers understand the characters. Dialogue usually makes the characters seem more real and interesting. Dialogue works, though, only if it sounds like a *real* conversation. Whether it's two aliens chatting as they zoom through space, or a girl complaining to her mother about having too much homework, the words and the rhythm of the conversation need to be *realistic.*

Sharing an Example: Heads or Tails

In *Heads or Tails,* twelve-year-old Jack is sure he's going to "get it" for his part in his brother Pete's bike accident. While you are reading, ask yourself, "Does this sound like a real conversation between a parent and a child?"

I hopped off the back of Frankie's bike, and when the fog drifted away, I found him. He had collided head-on with a mailbox on the edge of the street. He was lying in the grass with his good hand over his mouth. BoBo was whimpering and licking his face. "Let me see, let me see," I shouted. He lifted his hand. His left front tooth was chipped in half. "You might as well have my allowance for life," I said, sighing. "I won't need it where I'm going."

After dinner, Dad had come into my room and sat on the corner of my bed.

"What happened?" he asked.

I explained how I tried to keep Pete from following me.

"Did you ever think that you could have just turned around and led him home?"

"No," I said.

"Don't you think you should set a good example for him?"

"Yes," I said, feeling doomed.

"Then why don't you use your head, before you break it open like that Pagoda kid."

"Yes," I said again.

"Or before Pete breaks his head instead of his arm or tooth."

"Yes, Dad."

"I can't be here to watch over you kids all the time. When I turn my back, I count on you to use common sense."

"Yes, Dad."

"I don't want people talking about our family the way they talk about the Pagodas." He got up and strolled out of the room.

Jack Gantos. *Heads or Tails.* (USA: Farrar Straus Giroux, 1994) p. 116

Your Response

You've probably been in trouble with a parent or a teacher once in a while. Think about what you said and about what was said to you. Then decide whether this dialogue sounds like a father and son having a serious conversation.

_____ Yes, it sounded just the way a parent and child would talk.

_____ No, it didn't sound anything like the way real people would talk.

_____ I am not sure. I really couldn't tell.

Real Conversation, Dynamite Dialogue

Let's look at another example of dialogue and see how authentic it sounds. If you think that the dialogue isn't real enough, consider how you could change it to make it sound the way real people in the same situation would talk. Read the dialogue between Tessa and her dad on page 86.

Tessa and her dad were seated across the table having dinner. Her mom and baby brother had gone off to do an errand.

"Tell me, Father, how did things go for you at work today?" Tessa liked to be involved in her parents' lives.

"Fine," he said, like a door opening and shutting quickly.

"I don't wish to invade your personal space, but I was hoping to hear something a bit more specific." Tessa wasn't going to give up so easily.

"I said *fine,*" he answered, louder this time.

"Let's try it this way. How about telling me the highlights and lowlights of your day," suggested Tessa.

"OK, OK, *whatever!* If I tell you, will you just get off my back?"

Tessa could tell the situation was heating up. "I want you to share only if you feel comfortable."

Her dad stood up. "Fine! I had this really difficult client, OK? And he doesn't want to work with our company and stuff any more, right? So he tells me to chill. And it was just a bummer of a day. So, I'm like, well, whatever! There, are you *happy* now?"

Tessa knew that hadn't been easy for her dad. "I really appreciate the way you opened up to me," she said. "Thank you for sharing."

Do Tessa and her father sound like real people talking?

_____ Absolutely! That's the way parents and children always talk.

_____ No way! They aren't even close to sounding real.

If you thought this dialogue needed some help, you're right!

A Plan to Follow: From Dud to Dynamite!

Work with a partner to rewrite the dialogue. Choose one character (Tessa or her father), and have your partner take the other character. Decide which character will start the conversation, and have that person write one line. The other person will then write what his or her character would say in reply. Let the words flow back and forth, like a real father and daughter talking. Do not try to copy what is in the original paragraph. Just work on making Tessa and her father seem like real people talking about their day. Create at least six lines of dialogue—three lines each.

_____

_____

_____

_____

_____

_____

Share and Compare

When you have finished writing, read the dialogue aloud with your partner. Take turns reading each character's lines. How does the dialogue sound? Is it as smooth and realistic as when you wrote it? If the answer is no, change it again to make it stronger and more real. (Perhaps you and your partner will want to share your dialogue by reading it to the class.)

A Writer's Question

If someone asked you the secret to writing smooth, authentic dialogue, what would you tell that person? Write whatever suggestions you think will work.

Here are the secrets to smooth, authentic dialogue: _____

_____

_____

name: .... date: ....

Focusing on Fluency in Your Own Writing

You have had practice combining sentences to make writing smooth, varying the length of sentences to establish rhythm, and creating dialogue to make people and situations seem more real. You have read some examples of fluent writing, and you have revised some weak examples. That is a lot of work, but you have not yet had a chance to focus on the fluency of your own writing.

Select a Sample

Whether you keep your own writing in a folder, in a box, or in a secret safe behind a big painting on the wall, select a piece to be reviewed. Don't worry about whether the piece is an unfinished draft. You are looking for a sample of your writing that needs to be revised to improve fluency.

Share, Compare, Read, and Discuss

Next, you're going to work in a small group. Once you are in your group, take turns reading your writing aloud to the rest of the group.

As a responder . . . Your comments should focus on fluency. You can ask the writer questions or make suggestions about strategies to improve fluency. Make sure that any comments you make are aimed at supporting your classmate as a writer.

As a writer . . . When it's your turn to share, be ready to listen to your group's feedback and to accept any help they might offer. Make notes to help you remember helpful suggestions. Keep an open mind. Remember—someone making a suggestion doesn't mean your writing has no strong points! The purpose is to make your writing stronger.

Time to Revise

You have selected a piece of your own to revise, and you have shared and discussed your writing. Now it's time to get busy with your pencil! Put a check next to each of the following revision strategies you think might help your paper:

_____ Combining sentences—"Adding" short sentences together to create a longer one.

_____ Varying the length of sentences—"Doing the numbers" by counting the words in each sentence to see how much sentence length varies.

_____ Trying different beginnings—Starting sentences in different ways so that reading aloud does not get monotonous.

_____ Creating realistic dialogue—Making sure the conversation sounds like real people talking.

In choosing strategies that will work for you, think about the comments from your group. Read any feedback you received. Which strategies will make your writing stronger?

Share and Compare

After you have finished revising your writing, get together with at least one person from your original sharing group. Take turns reading your writing aloud. Talk about the changes you made. Tell your partner(s) what you liked about their revisions. Good revision always deserves praise.

A Writer's Question

How would you assess the fluency of your newly revised piece of writing? Rate yourself from 1 to 5, with 1 being the lowest and 5 being the highest.

1	2	3	4	5
There's more revising to do.				This writing is very smooth.

Unit 6

ConVentions

Do you ever take one last look in the mirror just to make sure that your hair is neat and your shirt is tucked in? As you're looking in that mirror, you might say to yourself, "Hey, I forgot to button my shirt!"

A good editor always checks a piece of writing for errors in conventions. He or she will look for mistakes in capitalization, spelling, punctuation, grammar, and so on. You might think that when it comes to writing a paper, these are small problems. But if you go out without buttoning your shirt, someone will notice, even if you usually look well-dressed. Errors in writing are like that, too. Misspell a word, and the reader will spot it—no matter how free of errors the rest of your text might be.

This unit will give you some tips for becoming a good editor. You'll learn about

◆ revising and editing

◆ identifying errors

◆ using editors' marks

◆ editing text

Lesson 21

Burgers, Granola Bars, Revising, and Editing

If you order a hamburger with the works and are served a granola bar, you might wonder how anyone could confuse the two items. Both the hamburger and the granola bar are foods, but the similarity ends there. In the same way, both revising and editing are part of the writing process, but are they just two names for the same activity? They are not. Each involves a different way of thinking and different strategies. Let's find out what you know about revising and editing.

First Impressions: What Do You Remember?

You've been a writer for a few years now, so let's start with two important questions: What is **revising?** What is **editing?** Write your first thoughts here:

Revising is _____

_____ .

Editing is _____

_____ .

All Together Now

Fill in the chart by turning your ideas about revising and editing into action examples: for example, **Revising/Editing** is *adding a missing period . . . adding new information about my topic. . . .* Each example should be something writers and editors do. (**Hint:** Revision involves *big* changes, like adding information; editing involves *smaller* changes, like putting in a missing period.)

REVISING is . . .	EDITING is . . .
1. Adding a sentence to strengthen my idea	Adding a capital to the name of a city
2.	
3.	
4.	
5.	
6.	
7.	
8.	
9.	
10.	

Your Response

Are the differences between these two terms becoming clearer? Look at what you first wrote about **revising** and **editing,** and then read through the table you and your class completed. Do you see any differences?

Revising and Editing in Action

Look carefully at the **Before** and **After** examples that follow. In each case, the writer has made some changes. Decide whether the writer was revising or editing. Explain your answer by listing some changes the writer made.

Sample 1

Before: Then, the recycling truck comes down the street to pick it up. Next, I have to put the box out by the curb the night before. First, I have to gather the newspapers, scrap paper, cans, and bottles.

After: First, I have to gather the newspapers, scrap paper, cans, plastic, and glass bottles. Next, I have to put the box out by the curb on Tuesday night so that it can be collected early the following morning. Then, on Wednesday morning, the recycling truck comes down the street to pick it up.

_____

_____

_____

Sample 2

Before: First, I have gather the newspapers scrap paper cans plastic, and glass bottles. next, I have to put the Box out by the curb on tuesday night, so that it can be collected early the following morning Then, on Wednesday morning, the recycling truck comes the street to pick it up.

After: First, I have to gather the newspapers, scrap paper, cans, plastic, and glass bottles. Next, I have to put the box out by the curb on Tuesday night so that it can be collected early the following morning. Then, on Wednesday morning, the recycling truck comes down the street to pick it up.

_____

_____

_____

Final Chance to Narrow It Down

Decide whether each of the following items is an example of **revising** or **editing.** Then mark your choice with an **X.**

1. Changing the lead in a report from "In this report about snakes, I will tell you how cool they are" to "You're waist-deep in water when suddenly a long reptile wraps itself around you. Meet the reticulated python, one of the many stars of the Wonderful World of Snakes."

   _____ **Revising**   _____ **Editing**

2. Combining some sentences to create a more fluent paragraph.

   _____ **Revising**   _____ **Editing**

3. Correcting the spelling of "graffiti" in a report on vandalism.

   _____ **Revising**   _____ **Editing**

4. Writing more than one ending and then deciding which one works best.

   _____ **Revising**   _____ **Editing**

5. Checking for capital letters at the beginning of every sentence.

   _____ **Revising**   _____ **Editing**

A Writer's Question

Review your first definitions. Then, consider your final ideas about revising and editing. Which of these two activities do you find more challenging?

name: .... date: ....

Developing Your Editor's Eye

In the final stages of the writing process, it is important to identify errors in spelling, punctuation, capitalization, and grammar. An editor's sharp eye will spot these errors. To develop an editor's eye takes practice, and it's often more helpful to practice on someone else's writing. Once you become skilled at spotting errors in others' writing, you will find it easier to spot the errors in your own writing.

A Little Warm-Up

With an open mind, open eyes, and an alert ear, read the sample sentence. Circle any errors you find.

I dont no what happened, but the end of the school year just sneaked up behind me and gave a kick. where did the Time go. i guess I don't understand people who say they the school. year moves slowly.

A Quick Count and Share

How many errors did you find? Write your total count here: ____ Compare your number with a partner's. If your numbers don't match, check the sentences a second time, and discuss what you find.

name: .... date: ....

Write the total number of errors your class found here: ____
How was *your* editor's eye? Did you find the same number of
errors as others found? You are probably ready now to use
your editor's eye on a longer piece of writing.

A Magnifying Glass for Your Editor's Eye

When you're looking for errors in someone else's writing,
does your editor's eye have a strategy? Here's a list of
editor's strategies that may help. There are a few blank
spaces in case you have an idea that we haven't thought of.

My Editor's Eye

1. Look closely at the beginning and ending of each sentence.
   This is a fast way to spot some of the most common mistakes
   writers make: leaving out capital letters at the beginning or
   forgetting end punctuation—period, question mark,
   exclamation point.

2. Read carefully for words that don't look or sound right.
   This is often a sign that a word is misspelled or used incorrectly.

3. Look for proper nouns (names of people and places, product
   names, and so on) that might be missing a capital letter.

4. Keep an eye out for "I." It's a fairly common error to use
   "i" instead of "I."

5. Look for commas to separate items in a list.

6. Make sure you used apostrophes in contractions or to
   show ownership. But remember—not every word that ends
   in *s* calls for an apostrophe!

7.

8.

9.

10.

Editor's Eyes Open: Ready, Set, Spot!

Ready for a challenge? Here's a longer piece of writing. Follow along carefully while your teacher reads it aloud. Circle any errors you spot the first time through. Read through the passage as many times as you need to, spotting and circling, until you're confident you have found all the errors.

My family is leaving for Italy on friday. It will be the longest I have ever taken and my first trip out of the Country. Were flying into the city of florence and then driving into the countryside to stay in a house. Im a little nervus, because i don't speak Italian I will try my best to learn some basic words to be polite and show them I'm trying. my plane is to keep a journal take lots of pictures and send postcards to all my frends. Ciao! (That's Italian for good-bye and sounds like "chow"!)

Total number of errors I found: _____

Florence

Share and Compare

Share your results with a partner. Compare your error totals. If you did not find the same number of errors as your partner, review the passage together for errors either of you may have missed.

A Writer's Question

How do you feel right now about your developing editor's eye? Rate yourself from 1 to 6, with 1 being the lowest and 6 being the highest.

| **1** | **2** | **3** | **4** | **5** | **6** |

My "eye" needs more practice.

My "eye" is sharp! I found all the common errors and most of the other mistakes, too.

name: .... date: ....

Clang the Symbols!

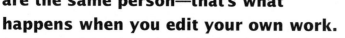

Members of a band express excitement with cymbals. Editors use "symbols," or marks, to communicate with writers. Each mark has a special meaning that tells the writer what needs fixing. Sometimes the writer and editor are the same person—that's what happens when you edit your own work. Putting editors' marks in your own writing is like writing little notes to yourself about how to correct your work.

Eight Editors' Marks

In this lesson, you will learn eight editors' marks. Use the chart on the following page whenever you need to. Remember, these marks are a fast way to say, "There's a mistake here. Fix it!" When you use them in your own writing, the message is just for you: *Add a period, use quotation marks, make this letter a capital . . .* and so on.

name: .... date: ....

Mark	Meaning	Use
1. ℘	Delete (Take it out.)	My dog is ~~the~~ my friend.
2. ∧	Add a word.	Pizza is ^{my}‸favorite food.
3. ≡	Capitalize this letter.	I live in p̲o̲r̲tland.
4. ⁄	Make this a lowercase letter.	My sister is Ø̸lder than I am.
5. ⊙	Add a period.	I am leaving on Tuesday⊙
6. ∧,	Add a comma.	I ate juice‸toast‸and cereal.
7. ⌄	Add an apostrophe.	The neighbor⌄s dog bit me.
8. ⌄⌄ ⌄⌄	Add quotation marks.	⌄⌄I'm having a blast,⌄⌄ he shouted.

A Little Warm-Up

For each item, "read" the editors' marks and write what they are telling you to do.

1. ⌄I don⌄t think I can go⌄Samane said⊙
   ‸

_____

_____

_____

2. she won't ≡ ~~Need~~ ^{to}∧ bring a coat.
   ≡

_____

_____

_____

3. My brothers need to ~~the~~ wash the car, mow the lawn, and sweep the driveway.

_____

_____

_____

You're the Editor, So Clang the "Symbols"!

Look for errors in the following passage. Use editor's symbols to tell the writer what needs to be done. You don't need to *fix* the errors. Just identify them.

Graduation Day

My older brother Graduated from high school last night. One of the the speakers said, Your actions will speak volumes about your character. I think she meant that people show who they are by they do. that was a pretty good message. There were three other Speakers who seemed to go on forever, and I cant remember what they. My brother and his friends sure looked relieved happy when they picked up their diplomas.

A Writer's Question

Think about your writing. Which editing mark do you think you will use the least while editing your own writing? Which one will you use the most? Is there a mark we haven't given you that you think you will need as an editor?

name: .... date: ....

Editing Is the Name of the Game

When you edit your own work or that of another writer, you have important work to do. You must have the right tools and the right attitude. You must know your editors' marks and be ready to identify errors. You will use your eyes to find the errors and your ears to hear the errors. Every time you edit, you want to get better with your tools and more alert with your eyes and ears.

Did I miss anything?

Getting Revved Up

One important part of editing is attitude. You need to understand the importance of the job and be committed to helping the writer. Here's a warm-up to get your eyes, ears, and attitude focused on the job. Quietly read the example aloud to yourself. Mark any and all errors with the correct editors' marks (use the chart from Lesson 23). You will compare your editing results with those of a partner when you have completed your work.

I thought Summer was supposed to be a the time of relaxation. my dad always says, Summer, the way I remember it, is all about kids bikes families sun and lots of time. Ha! my whole is taken up with lessons, camps, trips, and projects. School gets out on a Thursday, and my swimming lessons start on Monday morning. Monday afternoon is when soccer day camp Starts In between, we have this big yard project we all have to help to with. I think you get the idea. Summer!

Number of errors I found: _____

Share and Compare

Share your editing results with a partner. First, compare the number of errors you each found. Then check to see whether you found the same errors. Did you use the same editors' marks to indicate the errors? If you see anything you want to add or change, make those changes.

Number of errors my partner and I found together: _____

A Little More to Do

You should be ready to do a larger editing job. Check your **E.E.E.A.,** your **E**ditor's **E**ye, **E**ar, and **A**ttitude. Read the following passage aloud to yourself. As you find errors, mark them with the proper editors' marks. If you can't remember a symbol, refer to the chart on page 101.

Once a Month at school, we do very cool activity called Art Literacy. Parent volunteers come into the our class and tell us about a certain artist or kind of art They show us slides of the artists their art and even where they lived and worked.

sometimes, they have pieces of art to pass around. One of them said, This will give you a real feel for the art. the best part is the art activity, when we get to create something like the did, using the same materials, colors, and style. Last month, we learned about Aboriginal about art from australia. It was fun because we got to listen to some Music and heard stories that helped us understand the people and their art   I cant wait until next month.

Total number of errors I found: _____

Share and Compare

Share your editing results with a partner. How many errors did each of you identify? What kinds of errors did you find? Did each of you use the same editors' marks? If your partner found something you missed or used an editing mark you had forgotten, go ahead and make the correction. This practice is a team effort!

Total number of errors my partner and I found together: _____

A Writer's Question

After editing on your own and with a partner, which kinds of errors are you having a tough time spotting? Which ones do you spot every time?

name: .... date: ....

Wrap-up Activity 1

Traits: In Their Own Words

What if the six traits of writing were characters that could describe themselves in their own words? Do you think you could recognize them from the words they might use to describe themselves? Read the descriptions given by each trait character. Then, from the four choices, pick the trait you think is the best match. Put an **X** by that trait's name.

1. "I'm obsessive about correct spelling and punctuation. When I see examples of poor grammar, I cringe. Missing capital letters make me want to scream!"

   ___ Ideas   ___ Conventions

   ___ Voice   ___ Sentence Fluency

2. "I'm known for my individuality and strong feelings. When I am at my best, I have spirit, energy, and enthusiasm. I don't always sound the same, though. I can change, depending on my purpose. Writers everywhere depend on me to get and hold their readers' attention."

   ___ Ideas   ___ Sentence Fluency

   ___ Conventions   ___ Voice

3. "I hate disorder! I believe that events and actions should be in their proper places and should come at the right times. When I'm around, ideas are *never* disconnected. I like to start with a strong lead and finish with an equally strong conclusion."

   ___ Word Choice   ___ Voice

   ___ Organization   ___ Conventions

4. "I get a BIG kick out of verbs! They make me feel energized! Sensory words that describe sights, sounds, feelings, smells, and tastes are my favorites, too. I'm not a fan of inflated language, though. Writing should have a fresh, individual sound."

___ Word Choice   ___ Voice

___ Organization   ___ Sentence Fluency

5. "Natural-sounding dialogue is one of my specialties, and I make writing fun and easy to read aloud. I can begin a sentence in more ways than anyone else can. I love to blend long, smooth-flowing sentences with those that are short, concise, and to the point."

___ Word Choice   ___ Sentence Fluency

___ Ideas   ___ Conventions

6. "Some say that I am the heart and soul of writing—the very reason people write. Often, I carry the main message with me, and I tote a *huge* bag of vivid details. Each time I pull one out of the bag, readers are filled with delight!"

___ Conventions   ___ Organization

___ Ideas   ___ Sentence Fluency

Check your answers with a partner, and discuss how you answered each question. Were these traits easy for you to recognize?

___ Yes! We recognized every one.

___ We got stuck once or twice, but we knew most of them.

___ Oops! We didn't know these traits as well as we thought!

Wrap-up Activity 2

Making a Diagnosis

Sometimes a baseball team hits a losing streak. Game after game, they just can't seem to score any runs. The coach takes a closer look and begins to think, "Gee, the pitching could be stronger, the players aren't stealing enough bases, and too many hitters are striking out."

This coach is making a diagnosis—figuring out what the problems are. When you know the six traits, you can use them to diagnose writing problems, such as vague details, confusing order, lack of voice, or many run-ons. You then revise to get rid of the problems.

Read each of the four writing samples. Then decide what you think the main problem is in each sample. Circle *a, b, c,* or *d.* Write your own comments, too. (**Note:** A writing sample may have more than one problem, but one particular problem should stand out.)

Sample 1

My favorite food is spaghetti. I love sucking it up between my lips; but if my mom catches me, she makes me leave the table. When I was seven, my dad taught me to play football. He took this goofy picture of me wearing his helmet, which completely covers my eyes, so you can't even tell it's me. My sister likes to play cards, but I think that's about as exciting as trimming your toenails. Have you ever been white-water rafting? I have never actually been, but someday I'm going to go down the Colorado River. If you want the thrill of your life, though, you should try bungee jumping. That got my heart going so fast I felt like a human helicopter.

The MAIN problem with Sample 1 is

a. Ideas: The writer's message is not clear.

b. Voice: The writer does not reveal any personal feelings or put any energy into the writing.

    c. Organization: The order of events is confusing.

    d. Conventions: There are many errors in spelling, punctuation, and grammar.

My thoughts about Sample 1: _____

_____

_____

Sample 2

    It was a beautiful day. The sun was shining brightly. We went to the woods to hike. We met several friends there. We all brought picnic lunches. First, we hiked to the top of a hill. From there, you could see forever! Then, we ate our lunches. It was a great day! I'll always remember it.

    The MAIN problem with Sample 2 is

    a. Ideas: It is hard to tell what the writer is talking about.

    b. Organization: The part about eating lunch should come right at the beginning.

    c. Sentence Fluency: Too many sentences begin the same way, and they're all about the same length.

    d. Conventions: The spelling and punctuation errors make it hard to concentrate on the writer's main message.

My thoughts about Sample 2: _____

_____

_____

Sample 3

I think we should have less homework. The reason I feel this way is that homework is boring. In addition, you do not learn that much more. You do learn some things, but it is not worth it for the time you spend. A lot of my friends feel the same way. I think we should do more of our work right in school. Then we would not have that much homework. If we did not have homework, we could be doing other things. We could be playing outside or watching TV and stuff. Also, our parents would not have to help us with our school work and they might like that. So having less homework would really be OK.

The MAIN problem with Sample 3 is

a. Conventions: Too many words are misspelled.

b. Voice: The writer puts almost no energy or emotion into this paper.

c. Ideas: There is no main idea, so it's hard to know what the writer is trying to tell us.

d. Sentence Fluency: There are too many run-on sentences.

My thoughts about Sample 3: _____

_____

_____

Sample 4

When I landed my first fish, I was so excited! It was a huge salmon, and because I was only seven at the time, it weighed about half as much as I did! For a long time it was a contest whether I would pull it out of the river or whether it would pull me in. It all started when Dad woke me up at 3 o' clock in the morning. Believe me, it's no fun having someone shake you awake in the middle of the night. We used flies my dad tied, and he promised he'd teach me how to do it just the way he does. Dad said, "You catch the best fish with your own flies." We didn't even eat breakfast before we left. I could have eaten a doughnut, but Dad said, "If we're late to the river, we'll miss the big ones." Now I have my beautiful fish mounted and hanging on the wall where everyone can admire it. That fish put up a fight, but I won. The thing I remember best was how cold the river felt, even through my rubber boots.

The MAIN problem with Sample 4 is

    a. Sentence Fluency: Almost all the sentences begin the same way.

    b. Ideas: The writer supplies no details to help us picture this fishing adventure.

    c. Organization: The order of events is confusing and hard to follow.

    d. Voice: The writing is flat because the writer sounds so bored with this topic.

My thoughts about Sample 4: _____

_____

_____

Check your answers with those of your partner.
Did you diagnose the problem the same way?

_____ Yes! We diagnosed all the same problems.

_____ Most of our answers were the same.

_____ Oops! We didn't know these traits as well as we thought!